Best w
Marion Mm

service

Marion Husband
First published by
MUDFOG
July 2003

Mudfog
c/o Cleveland Arts
Melrose House
Melrose Street
Middlesbrough
TS1 2HZ

Tel: 01642 264651

ISBN 1 899503 54 ??

Design and layout by
Archetype Tel: 01642 384 576

Acknowledgements

Mudfog acknowledges support of
Cleveland Arts, Northern Arts Regional Lottery Programme, Middlesbrough
Borough Council, Stockton Borough Council
and the Northern Rock Foundation.
Mudfog is a member of the Independent Northern Publishers.

Contents

Foreward 5

On The Beach With My Bow-Legged Baby .7

Two World Wars 8

White 9

Home 10

Wedding, 1948 11

Day Trip 12

Father's Occupation 13

Wedding Day 1985 14

Baby Toys 15

Childhood Memories 16

Elderly Mentally Impaired 17

Dream 18

I Can't Give You What You Had Before 19

For Paul, c1917 20

Armistice, for Adam 21

Service of Remembrance 22

For my Dad, Ted Donkin, 1913 - 2003

No one's relationship with their father is entirely uncomplicated. I'm the second youngest of six children born to my mother and father between 1952 and 1963. By the time I was born Dad was forty-eight, a strong, energetic man driven to work punishingly hard by his need for security. My earliest memories of my father are of being shy of him, and although I was a timid child and shy of everyone, I felt I should be particularly wary of him, his quick and furious temper, his heavy-handed teasing, even his sweet, endless flattery. I was his little Mariarnnie, a name that in my childish fastidiousness used to make me squirm, suspecting as I did that he'd forgotten my real name. He used to pretend to be surprised to see me when he came home, as though he'd forgotten how many children he'd had and I was some stranger's child wandered into his house by mistake. On my seventh or eighth birthday he asked me how old I was, again (feigning?) admiring surprise at the achievement of another year. Perhaps he knew how old I was, perhaps not. Nowadays I look back and think it would be all too easy to forget. He was the busiest man I knew; I was proud of the fact he never watched television or went to pubs, proud too that he was so much older than most children's fathers, that he'd done more and seen more and hadn't given in.

His war stories, which some of these poems are based on, were told in a straightforward, linear way. He kept us waiting for the punch line, for his arrival in Durban to see the fat whites with whips, for Ginger to lose all his money to an Arab street vendor, for the water truck to be exploded. His sense of the injustices of poverty was heightened by his experiences in Palestine, India and South Africa. He was disgusted by the evidence of vast riches along side the kind of poverty that appalled even him, a young man brought up in Britain in the aftermath of the First World War. Hating racism, and never one to take much notice of propaganda, he loved the Italian prisoners of war for their warmth and vividness, sharing their passion for good food and their belief that the British and Germans loved war and were never happier than when chasing each other across continents.
He seemed ambiguous about the Americans he met, convinced that the USA won the war but astonished by its excesses. While he was pouring liquefied bully beef from its can the American troops were eating peaches

and cream. I remember the indignation in his voice as he told us this, the kind of scorn for the easy come, easy go American shrugs that could only come from a man whose own life had been anything but easy.

Dad didn't have much of a sense of Englishness, you could search his heart for a long time I think without finding much evidence of pride in his country. He never talked about missing home. He was stoical and tough and unsentimental, laughing at events that must have been terrifying at the time. 'I ran faster than the others, pet,' a part explanation of how he survived Rommel, who said, 'The ordinary soldier has a surprisingly good nose for what is true and what is false.' Dad was one such 'ordinary' soldier.

I grew to know my father better as a teenager, when he'd slowed down a little. I remember keeping house for him when my mother visited my sister in Canada and look back at the time as one of the happiest in my life. For all his energy he could be extremely relaxed, a calm presence smoking his pipe as he read the Gazette or watched a John Wayne war film or western on tv. Although as I grew older we clashed often, I felt that in the end, if I'd done my best and acted properly in his sights, he would have supported me. He allowed for mistakes, for ordinary failings, as long as you'd tried.

Dad was a butcher, a chef, an owner of fish and chip shops and a bed and breakfast. He tried his hand at breeding pigs and kept hens whenever the circumstances allowed. He would have loved to have been a farmer, caring for the beasts instead of transporting their bones and terrible offal around Teesside, from slaughter-house to glue factory. He didn't stop working in his garden until he was late into his eighties and dementia began to over-take him, wiping away his memory and ability to recognise us. At the end of his life I might just as well been that stranger's child. He kept his big, broad smile right until the end, though, still surprised, still flattered to see us.

These poems are for him, but also for me, a way of remembering. The love poems at the end, from I Can't Give You What You Had Before, stem from a novel I've just completed about the love affair between two young men during the First World War. But I think even these were influenced by Dad, his stoicism and acceptance of life's complications.

On The Beach With My Bow-Legged Baby

On the beach with my bow-legged baby
on New Year's Day
I take photos
thinking Mam & Dad wouldn't come
to Redcar in January

Redcar was kept for Summer
picnics of Libby's corned beef
and Lowcock's lemonade
and what would be the point in winter?

Summer Sundays
Dad pitches a tent
sets up the Calor gas for tea
unfolds the Sunday Express in the shade of the awning
But Calor gas PG tastes like experiments
there's unnerving sand in the Mother's Pride
worry over socks lost in rock pools
found full of shells and devils' toenails
there's sand between my toes for days

On the beach with my bow-legged baby
I remember Dad rolled his trousers to his knees
marbled shins revealed
only on Redcar beach
on those rare Sundays in July

Two World Wars

You never rated Vera Lynn
you said the Italians were great lads and
the Yanks won the war
you remember Yanks in a gum-chewing accent
you never chewed real gum
only Yanks, with fat wallets and good dentists, chewed gum

You had an idea about war
war was letters home to Mother:
thanks for jam and mittens and soap; war was
being eaten by lice, buried in mud, missing
presumed dead
Mother never presumed
The bastard's alive in sin
in Bruges or Brussels
You had your own ideas. They couldn't remember everyone
mud is so secretive, after all

This war is someone else's idea
In this war the minaret's song is more foreign than the enemy
in this war you are close to God's places,
Bethlehem, Jerusalem
his gardens and his tomb

The Virgin bows beneath her weight in gold
beggars pester
you keep your money,
make a little. Remember
beneath Ginger's shirt is a stencilled crucifix,
lily white against flame red
you think it should be enough for anyone. But
palm crosses are good business
you send him off in the water truck
protected by his talisman

You see it in your mind's eye,
that surprised leap
that nose-dive of metal
You see the exploding water like a plume from a fountain
You think of Ginger
not knowing what hit him

You think of Mother
and the garden going to seed

White

He looked like Bing Crosby
my Dad
like the young singer who sang
I'm dreaming
and a white widow in Africa wanted him
to stay with her, on her land
land that stretched for miles and miles
Such fertile land and beautiful
as Eden
where black men were called boys
and the sun beat down, white as a drum

The whites had whips
he told me
how they cracked at the boys' feet
When Dad mimicked the flat Dutch drawl
he could have been one of them

In the sun
he wouldn't have missed England, only his mother
who never knew how close he came
to being a widow's man
except

the whites had whips

Years later
I hear the disgust in his voice
bringing him home to me
clear as Crosby singing

Home

So, you came home
England as you left it
(cold in greys and greens)
In a garden gone to seed
grass grows too quickly

and the lawn mower's rusting
and the blades need sharpening
and the cold becomes white and blue as veins
It rains
and you sleep on the floor
(the bed's too soft)

Do you dream of Durban?
You saw the world through a war
Does it seem sometimes
as if it never happened?

Anyway, it's over
Months after VE Day, VJ Day
your brother dies
(gives in)

War wounds
(it happens)

After a while you sleep on the bed.

Wedding, 1948

Mam's brother
is Dad's Best Man
he's blonde, like her
bright
like her

Afterwards, at the party
Mam sings
choosing The Chocolate Soldier
so sweet
he can't believe how sweet she is
and young,
blonde
like unripe strawberries

The groom in his wedding suit
carves ham for his guests
generous, smiling
handsome as forties' film stars
although I never heard him sing
not once

*

Only silly songs
songs for children:
"If I had a horse,
a great! Big! Horse!"
Ride on his knee
higher, faster
until we're breathless

Day Trip

Me-Ian-and-Andrew
in the back of the van
can still smell the bones
their sacks
knobbly as knuckles
that yesterday filled this space
between driver's seat and rear doors

In the back of the van
we sit on old bedroom curtains
a print of hunted beasts
and cavemen running
spears poised
the ancient scene
failing to cover
the unchanged smell of bones

Me-Ian-and-Andrew
know not to mention bones
that anyway are forgotten
as Daddy drives
and the wind blows
Redcar's rotten-egg-stink
yellow as last year's sand
whispering amongst the buckets-and-spades
and the canvas candy stripes
of seaside paraphernalia

*

I found innards
once
in the coalscuttle
Dad laughed
I think I did, too

Father's Occupation

Not only bones
but pigs
live Large Whites
bigger than you'd think

In the allotment
behind Thornaby baths
our feral cats
cruise on Katie's Large White back
For warmth,
Daddy said,
Feline free-loaders

Not only bones
and pigs
but fish
and chips
In the Elizabeth Street shop
a queue forms
snakes round the door
for cod or haddock
professionally filleted

On my birth certificate
Father's Occupation
reads
Fish Fryer
no bones about it

Wedding Day 1985

We don't talk
in the back of the limousine
my hooped skirt
takes up the space between us
white rayon and the scent of roses
clenched buds in a tight bouquet

In the pocket of your hired suit
your speech
worked on
worried out
A brief speech
unaccustomed as you are

My veil covers my face
a reason, an excuse
for silence
Five minutes in a limousine
and the world has slowed
to dreaming pace

Five minutes
There is none of the
Are you happy?
Are you sure?
pantomime
We both know
both certain

Baby Toys

So, only silly songs, then
songs for children
How much is that Doggie
and Daddy wouldn't buy me
old fashioned songs with rascal words
round and round the garden
tickle-you-under-there

Running out of memories
I call my sister
ten years older, she remembers
the same stories I remember
the same authorised version of a life:
The Day The Shop Caught Fire
The Day He Cooked Rissotto for Grandma
The Day The Ghost Tapped His Shoulder

There are personal memories –
the deliciously rubbery pig my sister coveted
that smelt as new as Christmas
and belonged to the usurper
the new Queen of the Castle in Dad's arms

I tell her I remember being
Queen of the Castle
a usurper in my turn
and that Dad never told me I was too old for baby toys
I wish he had
In Canada my intrepid sister laughs down the phone
she doesn't know I'm serious

Childhood Memories

It's like you're three again
that lost child
photographed so rarely
no keeps of lock or tooth or shoe

No Baby's First for such a bad little boy
jumping on the dead for an undertaker's shilling
correcting rigor under hobnailed boots
Should I believe it?
Other stories:

Saving your brother from an on-coming train
Being thrashed with nettles by the guard
Slaughtering beasts in a butcher's back yard
Witnessing your mother's head-banging grief
A brother lost in a war to end war

On my desk is a photograph
my own children in a silver frame
on a silver beach
dressed in blues
you would've laughed:
called me your bonny lass
Am I?
Still?

now you've retreated,
surrendering my name

Elderly Mentally Impaired

I find you and another EMI
searching cupboards along a corridor
frowning over lost or dead or hiding
You thank god when you see me
perhaps I'm what you're looking for

We form a procession,
you, me and your comrade
trailing old women in our wake
One says you can wear her dress
Tell me? What goes on when I'm not here?

You tell me you're worried about the funeral
Who's died, Dad? Who's dead?
I shouldn't ask
useless anxiety, dogged as ever
severs connections, takes you further away

I try to bring you back
remind you of things to remember:
the smells of roast-beef Sundays
sweetpeas, bones and pigs
You ask me where that boy has gone

Dream

For the second time I dreamt about you
well again
and younger
taking pains with a chest of drawers

But you were cured
as though from any ordinary illness
fit and funny as you were at eighty
I heard your voice over the slide of drawers
saying you'd been ill
but better now.

Here's my confession:
I want you well so you can die
with proper shock and suddenness
with the wake-up drama of surprise
I want to be startled in the dead of night
Why couldn't you conform?

But this dreaming state you're in
it's better for you
a return to pounding silence
although I know you fought it
and you were scared for a while
the returning became easier, I think

I can't wake you
to say goodbye

I Can't Give You What You Had Before

(after Fiaz Ahmed Fiaz)

I can't give you what you had before
You exist so life is good
you are all and all the world's pain is nothing
is there anything in this world but you?
In your eyes beginnings have no endings
I think of us together and all
impossibilities become small
But it is impossible, only wishes
and love is just one hurt in a world of hurt
There is more in life

The past casts its shadow
made into the richest cloth
there are slaves in the marketplace
sold still soiled, still bleeding
men who pulled through from the heat of corruption
I see their wounds weeping but what can I do?
Your beauty holds me always
but love is just one hurt in a world of hurt
There are different joys beside this
and I can't give you what you had before

For Paul, c1917

If you think that God is watching, look away
don't catch his eye
don't smile in his direction
don't think he's charmed by indiscretion
or will indulge peculiar strays
we're sinners, you and I
cover my face with don't-care kisses
eventually he'll turn away

When you cry out – at that moment
when the bed yields to the fastness of sand
if you feel you might be dying
hold onto me
it's best we drown

When you're killed
and if they find you
I want you brought home, laid out in my place
I'll keep a vigil, weave a rose through your fingers
as flickering church candles cast doubt on your face

Armistice, for Adam

Surrender
hold up your hands, palms out, eyes front
I kill my prisoners sometimes
no false moves then, please

Lie still
keep your eyes, your mouth, your memory shut
I know our history backwards
no more talking, please

Sleep
learn from the chaos of well-trod dreams
I'll watch your breathing breathlessly
no more dying, please

What's left?
Let me hold you in blind-man darkness
I know my way too well
I know the answers, all of them
no more questions, please

Service of Remembrance

I waited until the widows had gone
the fathers and mothers and little children
the Bishop, the mayor, the dumb-struck heroes
I waited until all the words were said
the hymns sung, the names recounted
So I wasn't there to think
I knew that boy, and that one too
Went to school with,
Lived next door to,
Kissed in a mother's dark doorway
a hundred deaths ago

When the plaque was finally shown
I wasn't there to bow
or hold my hat against my heart
or count dull seconds down
Standing shoulder to shoulder with other,
bare-headed men
I might have caught an eye
might have sighed, or worse
might have thought of you
naked,
sleeping,
in my bed
such thoughts know their place

After the widows, in an empty church
I trace the measured inch of stone
where your name
– lately tripped from a Bishop's tongue –
is blank verse carved in gold